All the Hanging Wrenches

Also by Barbara Edelman

Dream of the Gone-From City

All the Hanging Wrenches

Barbara Edelman

Carnegie Mellon University Press
Pittsburgh 2022

Acknowledgments

The author is grateful to the editors of the journals in which some of the poems in this book first appeared:

Appalachian Lit: "Fireworks for the Whole of June," "After Ray Carver via John Straley"
Leon Literary Review: "Exoskeleton," "Otsego Street"
One: "Poem Including Definitions of Untranslatable Words & Lines Adapted from a Student's Essay"
Pleiades: "Beings Who Were Nancy in the Backyard and in the Dream"
Spillway: "January Light"
Talking Writing: "The Naming of Small Things"

Thanks are due as well to the members of my extraordinary writing group; to teachers with whom I've studied: Dorothy Barressi, Toi Derricotte, Lynn Emanuel, and Ed Ochester; to the many writers and friends who have supported my writing; and to the Hambidge Center for its community and workspace.

Book design by Mary Warner

Library of Congress Control Number 2022939400
ISBN 978-0-88748-682-1

10 9 8 7 6 5 4 3 2 1

for my siblings, Laney, Kalman, and Harry Edelman

Contents

III

IV

beautiful beyond belief at this passing
at this very passing moment that's just passed

—Wislawa Szymborska

I

The White Cat

Into a pool of streetlight, the white cat returns. It is New
Year's Eve in a southeast pocket of the San Fernando Valley.
Rain falls like spears. I open the barred door to this memory.
It's always white metal bars that frame the scene, that protect
me from evangelists and *traficantes*. When the white cat
returns, she is not scratched or matted but unscathed and
shining with the surety of finding me. The wind dies. Rain
falls like poles. It is raining cats and dogs. The cat steps out of
the rain and into my home. The dogs find their doors. Their
bowls. The bone people in caps and torn parkas huddle under
bridges, mouths full of nothing but prophecy.

The Train Poem

I teach you sleep
to the howl of a train:
first, it's a rhythm
at the base of dream
then the whistle's long call
at your bedroom window
to wide open summer,

Panama Limited
City of Miami
Chicago bound.

I teach you the ride,
allowance packed tight
in your back-jeans pocket,

the run between cars,
the sudden outdoors, the roar,
the platform's wobble,
field-rush and rumble, marvel
at the door popping open

to a hundred stories.
I teach you one story,
one side of a town
divided by tracks,
one leg of a north/south line, Illinois Central

you with your beautiful skins
and the mountain ranges
of your names,

you, the boy who hears God
in the pause of his stutter,

you, the girl
who feels cold from the one day
of terror cold.

I teach you stories
and the leap between them

from the car of white linen and buckwheat cakes

to the car of loud baby

to the planet of smoke

to the Pullman of fold-up berths.

I teach you the link and the pin,
I teach you the twentieth century
limited—towns asleep
through the ghost of your face,
the fields and their burdens,
the moon and its road of light
moving with you.

Fireworks for the Whole of June

The light's not draining
from the sky,
it's stiffening,
backing away.

And now the wan sky is skin
with something missing
underneath,

and now the bone sky's a field
of faces erased.

Mirrors everywhere—
in how the word you're thinking
shows up in the book
in front of you,

in the muffled, sporadic
punches into air
as night goes charcoal
that bring a smell of burning,

in a sky of circular explosions, like
multiplying molecules of virus,

in the way that,
on some maps,
North America's a headless, flightless bird
running west,
devolving into fragments
at its edges.

Blessing

In the eating of lamb chops, I said
thank you. I thought about the word
docile, the word *apostle*, the word
slaughter. I thought about *frisky*,
crispy, I thought about James Dickey
and the ewe like moonlight
listening for foxes.

I rolled the word *gambol* along the insides
of my cheeks, along the *roof! roof! roof!*
of my mouth. I crouched like moonlight,
glistening with fox teeth. I sprang
at the till for Australian chops.

I thought, "Never cook a kid
in the milk of its mother." Hence,
two sets of dishes, dental floss,
a set of spells.

(To be safe, though, two fridges, two stoves.
two houses).

Tibetan monks eat yak without yacking
yet pledge compassion for all animals.

I thought about Christina Rossetti:
"White sheep, white sheep / on a blue hill
When the wind stops, you all stand still."

Why do they have to be sheep, though?
They could be cream puffs. De-animate
the metaphor before you eat it.

Little lamb, who made thee
juicy? From a tube, soon, in a lab, yes!
Then, happily, will I eat thee.

*

I saw the black cow grazing near the trail.
I saw the yellow ear tag.
I saw the bulk of body, the oak-bone eyes,

the lake eyes, moon eyes,
boulders-at-the-end-of-time eyes.

Sister Bovinia, if ever I should broil you,
let me wear a bit and bridle. Let me dream
the dream in which I eat my cat.

I say, forgive me. I say
give me. Cushion my bones.

Haven't you known this, too,
Ruminant? You in your chewing?
This noose, this loneliness?
Let me stroke your flank.
There are no eyes like yours.
My heart is a broken bottle.

To the Rowhouse Town

And there were all the blues
of lake and sky
your hand on the tiller

and icehouse blue
in the green coal valley
where you hid with your twin
in the thick of August
and fatherless blue in the rowhouse town
and moneyless blue and illness blue

Jew blue to the stooge
on the elevated train
in the city of higher ed

and cobalt blue of the ink that leaked
on the pocket of the jumpsuit, army green—
green suit of the war
suit of the workbench and wall above it

bench of the screws in their perfect compartments
the drill on its ear
the anvil like an armadillo

and all the hanging wrenches

We flew to the fatherless province
once, just we two
to the rowhouse town
of mother and mother and mother
when I was a feathery string bean child
child with the bitterest breath
a wild onion eater

and you were the father lost in a bookshelf
father diminished to shadow
to the dybbuk in the pine-paneled corner
to the tree in the etching
of *Susanna and the Elders*
to the print of Jesus
as a Hasid or a Turk

Father! Is that you inside the tallis?
Who are you mumbling to?
Is that you in the Smith Corona?
In the 78 of *Kiss Me Kate*?
In the dry sherry bottle?
Can you hear my blue voice?

You heard something
and it must have been me
You gave me a book by Diane di Prima
and one by John Ciardi
(You hung out with him at parties)

And when I was small, you read me to sleep
in a storm-deep voice—
into blizzards, hurricanes
islands and caves
I stayed awake

for the voice
even more than the story

You kissed me goodnight
in the middle of my forehead.

Beings Who Were Nancy in the Backyard and in the Dream

The blond doe behind the house was Nancy
and she held my gaze too long for a healthy deer
so I knew how things were
even before she dragged the crushed
leg away like a dead animal she was
hauling home.

And then the hammer-snout Siamese
with his flat stare was Nancy
and the girls in denim at the mirror with
mascara wands who would meet
no eye but their own
were Nancy
crowding the bathroom that was Nancy's

and the blond nanny in the kitchen who looked me
full on was just one
letter off and so,
of course, also Nancy

and the poet Joy Katz who had moved next door
though she resembled her dachshund
was in this case One Who Takes Joy
in Cats and thus, Nancy, too

and the action figure with the big head
and the geriatric poodle-baby
and my mother (forgive me)
and the fawn alone in shade beneath the fir tree.

The Naming of Small Things

1)
I've slept so well here at the sill
of open window, pillow nearly touching
the screen. This land is rain forest, charged
by rhythms of cicadas, riffing in and out by
day then blasting symphonic into darkness,
from tymbals in the abdomens of courting
males, a pattern that repeats and repeats
until I listen for variations in pitch, in
accent; variations within variations,
the wide night calling out
sleep brilliantly, pay attention.

2)
One more night before I drive back
into infuriating news. Yesterday, lost
on an unblazed trail, I hiked into a
rhododendron tunnel so long I ended up
in a neighboring state. A small fear
burrowed in me like a tick. I kept yanking
webs from my face and arms. The galls
on oak trees made me uneasy.

3)
Tonight—a crash near my head.
I sit up, believing, on the trail
out of sleep, that a bear hurled itself
against the cabin wall. Did I leave
food out? No other sound. A branch
must have fallen on the roof and remained.
What makes me think then of the pain
at the tip of my months-old incision,

ignored for weeks? I touch it. The intruder
lump, cut out, has re-emerged. In the fat
of my calf. Strange for a supporting limb
to share the name of a baby animal.

Poem Including Definitions of Untranslatable Words & Lines Adapted from a Student's Essay

My student is thin
like a shirt without a body,
a ribbon of skin.

From the river of her language
her ideas filter into English
until her words are *the amount of liquid you can cup
in one hand.* She sighs and her voice is
the road-like reflection of a moon

on water. Silver moon, cobalt water.
Voice divided as moonlight through the leaves
of old books, abandoned
in an abbey with no roof. She builds
sentences like streets in a city razed by fire.

Commuovere, I want to say, for I am
moved in a heartwarming way

when she translates the ancient
poet whom she does not name:

"In the past, the horses moved slow,
The carriages moved slow,
And so the letters between people moved slow.
You could have but one lover in a lifetime."

*

In Mexico
I moved slowly
through *still* and *not yet* and
not anymore.
We walked late into night
on uneven streets.
Our hands spoke, and sometimes
closed, as if to cup
the necessary word like water.
On the road between languages
my mind opened
like a roofless abbey.

*

New moon, purple sigh. Voice like
light on water. Though she is nineteen,
the student who translated
the ancient poet writes,

"The world moves too fast now for love."

* *Translations of untranslatable words are from* Lost in Translation *by Ella Frances Sanders, Ten Speed Press, Berkeley.*

White-throated Sparrow

The word that's gone
for example
could be *handkerchief*
and I'd think
Desdemona or *bandana,*
the cloth square sailing
without a name

It could be *Maamoul*
and the mind's powdered sugar
would find no place to settle

I have lost my *Maamoul*
and my Mamá
and the accent on the second syllable
the ear for cadence

It hovers like a moth
The word is moth
The word is mother
The mother hovers, still
though she is dead
Unstilled, she hovers in the heat

Though she is dead
she is buying me a car
and this buying makes her happy
happy in the part of my body
where she's stored
like a scroll inside a cartridge

In a car along a ridge
windows open
looking down on
fields of alfalfa
forests of hardwood
I'll be moving in her gift
She'll be still
beneath the fields

And the song
to me inaudible
that isn't really gone

for example
the white-throated sparrow
there's a terror
in the sound I cannot hear
as it embroiders the air

I am heir to a deafness
to a hardness, to a car
to a ridge above a farm
a farmhouse synagogue
a pewter tea set
a coil of roots.

II

Otsego Street

I left the alley and its dust. I left the white cat who was already gone. I left the talkative crows, the smell of weed. I took the bruise of theft. I took the cat-piss smell of eucalyptus, smell of smog, smell of self, smell of flatland dwellers on days when your sweat evaporates before you see it, when the circular valley is a furnace and you conserve your movements like money, you walk as if you had no bones, you walk as if the air is water, though the only water is in the spiked scales of cacti or escaping through the pores of your skin.

January Light

Jim's back from Panama, infused with umbilical
stem cells to bolster his immune system.
He'll see results within six months, if.

He's telling Paul and me about the monkey-viewing
ride on Gatun Lake, about the natural history
of north joining south: Three million years ago

the continents touched fingers. The cougar, porcupine,
opossum, and armadillo strolled down the isthmus
in The Great American Interchange of species.

It's twenty-one degrees and windy in the hills we
walk. Jim knows nothing about the donor whose cord
binds him to the southern hemisphere. The sun

bobs up twice and dunks back into clouds. I might have
kept my face deep in pillows this morning but for friends
who coaxed me into the cold. We hike with poles so not

to slide on icy trails. Paul reads a frozen patch of ground
for the story of last night's precip: rain, then freezing
rain, then snow. All I see in the clouded ice are circles—

zeroes, open mouths, apostrophes:

O friendship,
O winter light,
O miracle umbilical.

Into Air, Into Water

It was a moment that got away from her,
    a moment she got away on,

a car that might have braked at the sea cliff
    but didn't
        and took flight—

Mind like brushfire,
    inscrutable photographer,
        singer, mentor,

It was a life that got away from her
    and one she got away with
        for a while—

migration west to cantilevered houses
    touching sunsets,

a sun that took its sugarhold
    on all beneath it
        until it dropped, loaded
            into the ocean,

the friends who descended like grasshoppers
    onto deck chairs and steps,

the herd of children stampeding into the pool
    clutching stupid-faced, inflated horses

    while adults darkened into their alcohol
    and the so-good husband strummed
        an adulterous love song.

It was a brushfire that got away from her.

I think of the clown suit she donned
        for lunch with her ravenous therapist.

I think of the beauty of the two children, dropped
        at a friend's on the way to the cliff.

I see them holding hands
        the way they did when they first moved from New York,
        the sides of their small bodies touching.

The Bus

after The Bus *by Frida Kahlo*

The bus before the accident
is stilled into a place of waiting,
with blond wood floors
and a bench
from which the six, seated
people will not
rise—their feet too small
to support their bodies.

A nursing baby will not pull away—
its head an extension
of the mother's breast. She wears
colors of the earth. The bag
at her feet blooms
like a huge vegetable.

A young boy kneels at the window
with just a sliver of face,
his heart in his back.

There is beauty in the roundness
made of light
in breasts and knees,

some kind of patience
in the face of the laborer
with his necktie and denim overalls

who holds a tool that might
be squinted into a weapon
or a paintbrush.

Only the well dressed know
movement: blurred ears of the ginger
gringo with his bag of money;

flowing scarf
of the chic woman to his left
(some say she is Frida)
whose webbed right hand
covers the left.

But the poorer Frida
at the bench's other end
has been given the solidity
to hold this moment still.

Among the women, only she
has distinct fingers.

Lot's Wife

"Arise, take thy wife, and thy two daughters that are here; lest thou be swept away in the iniquity of the city. Escape for thy life; look not behind thee,"
—Angels to Lot, Genesis: 19

"But his wife looked back from behind him,
and she became a pillar of salt."

I was drowsing through Sunday school
to Mrs. Schiff's twang, dreaming
that I fled the burning city
in a long robe and sandals
with a family and a few goats.

That salt pillar
jolted me from my snooze.

Sammy Kane called Mrs. Schiff
Old Vacuum Cleaner Nose. Sammy
was truly bad. God would have turned him
to salt whether he looked back or not.

Through the classroom window,
I watched one cow grazing
on the far side of the parking lot.
I was thinking Lot was an odd name.

I was inhabiting the horror
of becoming a salt pillar, white
as a giant cigarette. Going from girl
to salt. Not me anymore.

And if an antelope were to lick me,
I wouldn't feel it.

I thought how I loved the fullness
of being me.
And now I look back

to see that recognition,
that love,
was the lesson I took
from the salt pillar tale

and I scrapped the one
that says, Choose
between blind obedience
and obliteration.

*

We flee from our city like thieves.
How can I help but look back
to see it burning as if struck
by lightning, the whole desert aglow
with its heat, tumbleweed aflame, rolling
towards us like a giant head on fire?

Why did I disobey, you ask?
Why did I look back?
Why are those the questions?

Why don't I have a name?

Camp Two

Consecrate the memory
of the crippled children's camp,
Camp Two,
where they bussed us on weekends to eat,

we normal ones,
those humid Junes in Southern Illinois
when the Camp One mess hall closed
and a few of us stayed between sessions.

Consecrate the woods, the paths,
the ramps to the Camp Two mess hall.

They split us up, the Camp One kids, one
to a table.

Consecrate the wheelchairs and metal braces
the shortened arm,
toothpick leg,
the hand curled
like a seashell.

Did I cower and stare?
Did I ask anyone
their name?

Or how they felt
about our cautious occupation
of their meals,

we of the four functioning limbs,
we of necks

that held our heads up, barely able
to eat in their presence,

stiff witnesses to innovation—
the first outdoor rec camp
of its kind in the nation?

Did they have secret names for us?
Consecrate the names.

Consecrate the cabins we returned to,
the bunks we climbed up to,

artillery of rain on tin roofs,
lightening gigantic as a bible
miracle,
eviscerating thunder,

and the luxury of shared terror:

Mad Myrtle out there with her axe
in the thickness of hills.

With the fine concentration
of the already dead,
she could track us by our whispers

and drag us from the cabin
to hack our perfect bodies into pieces
in the exquisitely dripping darkness.

Beach House, Circa 1967

for Liza, Matthew, & Katie

On the morning of the sick baby sea lion,
we glimpsed its silhouette
through fog. It would be
hours before the haze
burned off, before the world
gained shape and contrast: cliffs
and houses, pelicans and rocks, a tanker
far from shore. At that hour, lines
between air and sea and land
are tenuous: the universe
a thunder-blur of cloud
and surf. Slinkies of foam
through shifting patches of light.

As the world grew visible, we saw
how small it was, and weak—
long nosed, thin, and oily black.
Nancy, in a swimsuit and gray
sweatshirt, carried the pup in her arms
to the house. On the screened porch
we made a bed for it on blankets
beneath a quilt that it shook off.

She must have guessed it would not
live, and yet she fed it with a baby
bottle, massaged it,
called her vet and wept. I was fourteen.
I'd never seen a human
cry for an animal she'd just met.

My Father Visits Me in Sydney, Spring 2020

The roots of Ficus rise
into hallways higher than my head.
Sharp drop beyond the root walls
to water. The bay is indigo,
dimpled, white-laced by wake.

Sulphur-crested cockatoos in half flight
screech like crazy babies.

One hovers near my ear then perches,
white quilt of feathers,
yellow crest unfurled
to form an open hand.

I'm touched by flutter
and think *breath*.
The face beneath the crest
becomes familiar, tender.

"Why are you a bird, Dad?"
I'd have guessed dolphin, maybe
whale, something gentle and of water.

I hear an answer in his own, low
voice, from his face inside the bird
face, his mind before the lost mind.

"You know I loved wind."

On afternoons the Midwest sky went
greenish, he led us to the yard to see
the scalloping of clouds that might
portend tornadoes. It was eerily still.
When sirens sent us to the basement
he'd walk back out to watch the sky.

In the end, how he labored
toward this grace of hollow bones,
pushing a walker squashed onto tennis balls
the length of driveway,
the short wing of sidewalk,
the return. An hour's work.

High swish of wind in the ficus.
Slap of waves against the sea wall.

"Be careful," says my father
and rises on my exhale.

He flies above the harbor,
above the opera house and bridge,
above the cruise ship moored,
its crew marooned two weeks,
above the low sun bouncing
off the disinfected glass.

Darling Harbour

Is this the last innocent meal,
in Australasian sun,
long table on a gray wharf,
creak of moored boats?

The students are bored
by the National Maritime Museum

but not by lunch,
not by the lick of sea breeze,
not by cappuccino
with a chocolate anchor
sprinkled in its froth.

It's weeks before I'll hear a German
tourist on the metro call the virus
a conspiracy of Trump and Putin,

weeks before the prime minister
roars onto my screen, his head
the size of a garage door: "Stop
hoarding!" It's UnAustralian!"

Weeks before there's any talk of bodies.

Right now rain is the worst thing
we can imagine and we can't
really imagine rain.

And green-eyed Ella turns out
not to be rich
and to have worked
to fund this semester herself,

And round-faced Travis
becomes quietly nice,

and in five weeks they'll be locked
in their bedrooms, chewing
on the drawstrings of their hoodies.

After Ray Carver via John Straley

What if I said the word *scream*
and typed the word *sweet*
and hit send?

Would you think of summer—
bike trail through a canopy
of pine, brown needles laced
across asphalt,

and then the drape of rain
that makes its own
element, and white mist
rising from the creek?

Would you think of cycling
through darkness, the discs
of your wheels lit like moons?

Would you think
of all the languages
in which you know the words
for day and night?

I know I manufacture more anger
than my body can outride.
And that my body of anger
needs its own garage. And that
garage is just one *B* away
from garbage.

But as I write you, the sky
begins to soften its way to darkness,
pinkening in increments
against new-leaved trees.

The Intercontinental Bird Threat

Let us ban the Blackpoll Warbler, then—
who drops in to feed along our east coast
en route to Nova Scotia from Colombia.

It's the size of a fist, its song so creepily
high not all of us can hear it. It wears
a yarmulke. On return, it soars like a goblin
three days above the ocean without stopping.

At very least, let's make the warbler pay a toll—
the New York City bridge model:
hefty fee to enter; fly out free.

The witchy Frigatebird can play the updrafts
with such acrobatic tact it will ascend
half a mile above the Atlantic
without flapping. Let us ban it.
Its pterodactyl wings are freakish.

Let us ban the Arctic Tern for its black cap and cloak.
Let us ban the Northern Wheatear, who crosses ocean, ice,
        and desert.

Let us ban the Bar-tailed Godwit, that flying softball,
that inflates itself with fat, enlarging
its organs, then shrinks them back
in flight: feasting, as it pumps its wings,
on its own liver and kidneys; flying nine thousand
miles, nonstop, Alaska to New Zealand.

All that is fantastic, let us ban!

Better yet, let us empty the sky.

Let us crucify the Godwit,
        Let us bear it on a bier drawn by four oxen.

Let the Godwits
        be dropped into martyrdom,
        let them rain like dark coins,
        let their bodies clog the water meadows.

Let us hunt down the warbler, its notes
        so pure they hurt us
        like icicles in sunlight.

Let us seek it out with drones,
Let us roll in the tanks,
Let us unmake the warbler,

its body the size of a child's hand.

Our Bodies

Our bodies followed us around like the sky.
Few questioned our penchant for evaporation.

We aspired to be whispers, mothlike on our true
path to disappearance. As if some customized

Rapture, like a Shop-Vac, would guzzle us up
if we were thin enough, and if not, leave us

flattened like houseflies. In locker rooms
the bodies of the lovelies glowed like fish

bone. They moved within the *Followspot*
of our envy. Blessèd are the starving mice

that eat their own tails. Blessèd are the kneecaps,
unveiled, like the bald heads of babies. Remember

when we pulled away from ourselves like riptides?
Remember when we lived on pomegranate seeds,

and our mothers bargained our release? Hauled us
back into the land of gin and tonics, of Eames

chairs and the glass party table, of cigarettes
arranged in a silver top hat and cow tongue

on a green, ceramic plate? Of red-faced adults
with bloat-white voices who cornered us

between the kitchen and bathroom? And we
sought to weigh less than mosquitoes.

III

Cigarette

A man wields a lit cigarette like a knife, inches from a
woman's neck. He backs her down a sidewalk on a side street
on the Southside. He is ash-white, thin like smoke—gray hair,
gray clothes, gray teeth. She is skinny-white as a cigarette—
straw hair, cracked lips, burn coming close to her paper skin.
I have stopped my car. I climb out and bark, *Hey!* They snap
me a look. I am new to this city. My friend in the passenger
seat whispers *Get back in the car.* I yell *Hey!* again, and both
strangers glance at me, sidelong, fast, then pop back as if
elasticized to latch back onto one another's stare. *Do you want
me to call the cops?* I ask the woman, though it's years before
I'll own a cell phone. They hold, split second, he lowers the
ember of his weapon an inch and pauses, then advances it
toward her bare shoulder. *Do you want me to call the cops?* I say,
louder. She makes a noise that forms around the letter N and
vibrates as a grunt in her throat. She shakes her head. I am
a blip, an inconvenience, a danger. I get in the car and drive
away with my belief in cops.

Constitution, November 2018

Asked to write about
the Constitution, all I can
think of is my own
constitution and its latest
noises

and that after tragedy
in a sanctuary friends inhabit weekly
I moved quickly out of sorrow

into thinking some responses
to the shooting pissed me off.
"Everything pisses me off,"
I told a friend who called
from California.

"That sounds like a natural
response," she said, which
did not piss me off

but the words *natural* and *response*
sat next to each other like
blocks of wood and refused
to mean anything.

After mass murder
in the space where I prayed
once a year,
I continued fully
constituted

ligaments and tendons,
phone calls,
complete sentences,

I continued
what the framers of the constitution
might have called
my daily constitutionals

through this year's autumn—
that late bloomer.

I'm grateful to be
above ground in autumn
which is also the name
of the ten-year-old across the street

who put up the first
No matter where you're from
we welcome you in three
languages to our neighborhood.

Yesterday my university
held a memorial
for the shooting victims.

They gave out T-shirts
with a star of David dotting
the i of one word.

"*Shield* of David,"
the rabbi explained
"is the *true* meaning
of *Mogen David*,
signifying God as protector."

They had only extra-large shirts left
but I took one, thinking I might find
a large student, alone and scared

in the second month
of his first year
on this enormous campus
who might feel warmed
by the gift of a T-shirt.

And thinking of the large student
and his T-shirt
and its tiny shield
is the thing that made me cry.

Exoskeleton

Each trek has its own syntax.
My home on my back. My Quasimodo
shadow. I'm a slow beetle. Destination the top
of a mountain, the Milky Way's
veil and the silence. Each time I wake
there's a new sky. The Earth
spins faster up here.

Each time we rest in the desert,
I sleep; each time I sleep I dream
in stick figures. We are lower
than ocean. I slog across a ridge
to bury my dung. Night brings
an anarchist wind. The tent is a flight
risk. Under the Milky Way's map,
I dance on a sand hill
like a beetle on its dung ball.

Beneath the canoe, a school of dying
salmon. They rot as they swim.
Their disappearance begins on the inside.
They'll become the river and the banks
of the river and food for the fry
of their fry. At the falls where they leap,
one Grizzly eats only
the skin. Gulls take the flesh.

Once, I lived beneath a mountain range
of roofs. Pigeons
stood watch on the shingles.

Once, I lived in a sweet stucco box
with vines at the windows, spiders
in the vines, guitar in the alley,
salt on the wind.

Visitation During Solo Lockdown

After seeing the photo of D in his black sports coat—
a rose gold glow from his face
that traveled the circumference of his round pate—

I thought of astronauts who say the sight of earth within
the black of space defined their inner
orbit: that's how I felt about D's head in that moment.

I dreamed, of course, he was the one to save me, though
even to dream was to be saved.
I had wanted the Felliniesque pandemic dreams

everyone else was having, but that channel kept
eluding me. In this sleep, though,
I arrived, in color, at some home of D's with stairs

curving upward from the entryway. I stood halfway
up. His hair was black.
He brought me down a contraption wrapped in plastic,

a red, squid-like pouch with tubular arms and clamp
hook-ups. I thought, too,
of udders. *It's a cheap one*, he said. No sacrifice, he had

others, this giver of books turned giver of life-saving
gizmos. Then I stood alone
on a wood floor among shoes. A single, spike-heeled sandal—

dressy, black, very long; another in shiny red, toppled
on its side. I hadn't wanted
there to be a woman. A tall one. And then the child-shoes—

doll-tiny, unmatched and strewn. Grandchildren? Do they live
here? I wanted then to learn
how he and others constructed their lockdowns. What/if the logic.

But even in the dream I recognized these shoes to be
a past I lacked. A fullness
of life that rose up through the floorboards.

The Frontier

My father's face into a red
stump, his voice
to an animal growl,
my father's legs into chopsticks,
his fork into a soup spoon,
his soup onto the napkin
propped below his chin;

his book into a prop,
his prop plane to a sailboat,
his lake into open
ocean as a squall blows in
across the starboard bow.

I leave him in it
to tack into white caps, hand
on the tiller,
reading sky and gray water,
once again among the explorers
he loved.

Simile

At Costco, there's plastic like glass, plastic like wood,
plastic like flesh, plastic like metal, plastic like
plastic, cherries like cherries but a little bit like plastic.

A handsome poet once asked me, "Why don't
you write this line as a direct comparison? Not
'She had a face like an apricot muffin' but 'Her face

was an apricot muffin.' Because nothing is really *like*
anything else, is it?" He smiled like butter. He smiled
as if the beauty of his own face made his assertion

logical. That was a long time ago, before Costco entered
my poems, before I knew plastic entered animal guts.
My poems were full of webs and water bugs. I wondered,

is there currently a movement against similes? Nothing
is really *like* anything else but something really *is*
something else? The next day I wrote the word "Simile"

on the blackboard. The fourth graders read it as
"Smile." Some of them clapped and jumped up
and down. They wrote similes like boomerangs.

They made me smile so deeply my bones felt like
teeth. I've similed my way out of more than one situation.
"You should simile more often," a man used to tell me.

He was like another man who used to tell me the same
thing. He also said, "You have a simile like no one else's,"
though in fact it's very like my sister's and my niece's.

A simile is like a smile with two chameleon
eyes, scoping in two directions; or like a stretched
smile—a smile that goes on like a river.

Today on the Car Radio

someone said research conducted by someone somewhere
concluded that talking to yourself is a good thing.

"Excellent news!" I said to the radio.

I'm in the hills of Georgia for two weeks, alone in a
dilapidated house with no internet, cell service, TV, or radio.

"People with higher IQ's tend to talk to themselves," said
the car radio. "Talking to oneself does not indicate that one
is crazy; rather it improves focus, alleviates anxiety, and
facilitates working out problems."

What a relief. Especially since a few days ago, the car radio
told me loneliness takes several years off a person's life.

"Well, define loneliness," I'd said to the radio.

When I had a cat, I chatted with her despite her clear look of
boredom.

When I'm with another person, I sometimes feel we're both
talking to ourselves.

A rather pretty flying insect alighted on the pine table this
evening to join me for dinner.

"I question whether I'm actually lonely," I said to the insect.

Triad Artists Agency, Century City, 1980s

I had an assistant. Well, it's true, I had a series
of assistants. I called them assistants not
secretaries because I'd recently *been*
an assistant who did not want to be called
a secretary. This assistant
was Kenneth, scrubbed as a Polaroid
with a run-about eye.
To butter me up, Kenneth assigned me
a whole runway of celebrity look-alikes.

He saw me as the middle layer
in his success sandwich.
He wanted a better job and to begin with,
my job.
He wanted my window office, my
flowered couch, my
distant slit of ocean on days without smog.
Kenneth was subtle as a foghorn,
but that kind of swagger,
in men, was an asset.

"Cher," he said. "That's it. You remind me of Cher."

"Cher," I said, in a Cher deadpan. "But what about her willowy
neck, her chorus girl legs, her arms like garden snakes?"

"Facially," said Kenneth "and in your mannerisms."
He placed his chin on his manicured fingers
and assessed me: "Like Cher, only prettier."

I imagined dressing as a luna moth, à la Cher,
but worried I'd sprain my ankle
on the spiked heels. Driving to and from work,
I sang, "Baby don't go," Sonny's part, too, though I admit
I could never tell their voices apart.

I'd been trying hard
to make use of my expense account,
under pressure from the partners to schmooze more.
There were so few buyers, as we called them,
that I wanted to eat with,
but I took one I liked one to lunch—Charlie—
who booked Dick Clark specials.
Charlie said Dick had undergone so many face-lifts
it raised the philosophical question,
Could Dick's face
still be called Dick's face?

"Do I remind you of anyone?" I asked Charlie.
"You look *exactly* like my ex-wife," he said.

I looked exactly like a lot of ex-wives. Was it
possible, even in Hollywood, that all these men
had been married to the same woman?

Back at the office, Kenneth
was eating a corned beef sandwich
at his desk. "Christine Lahti"
he pronounced, "that's it," as if answering
a question that appeared in a bubble above
my head, or as if, in this culture of approving only
that which closely resembles
what's already approved,

I could not exist
without his comparisons.

"Christine Lahti," I said to Kenneth and his
sandwich. "Right."

Her hair like soft tumbleweed. Her lithe body
so different from mine. The certainty emanating
from her supple bones that she was Christine Lahti.

I rented all her movies. I hennaed my hair
slightly redder and let it curl forth.

Modern European History

Let a man find himself, in distinction from others, on top
of two wheels with a chain—at least in a poor country like
Russia—and his vanity begins to swell out like his tires. In
America it takes an automobile to produce this effect.

—Leon Trotsky

Mrs. Ralph, if not for you, I might have
slumped in the hallway for a year.
Instead, I read when I couldn't sleep.
Instead, I tied an Indian cotton scarf
around my forehead,
put on my green uniform
(jumper with a pleated skirt)
and stood before the class
with something like joy,
without longing to dissolve into water or woods,

and gave my talk on Trotsky
from three by five notecards—
his rise and his exile to Mexico,
his belief that only change endures, his theory
of permanent revolution.

Above me, the globe on a bookcase,
to my left, high windows
and your round face, smiling,
in front of me, the girls who scared me,
who could negotiate cities and makeup
and subways and boys,

who could break rules and swing their hair and lie,
who'd boarded together since middle school,

who'd lived in this secret America since birth,
in houses the size of the Petrograd palace,
amid social rituals I'd thought belonged
to the nineteenth century,

who were welcoming to me:
senior-year-imported hick from Southern
Illinois, reading to catch up on something
I couldn't identify.

Behind me, a blackboard and a desk
I sat down on. Behind me, the swells
of modern European history
you launched us into. You were
the questions and the doubt
inside the answers.

And when Stalin's assassin, with his ice axe,
hacked Trotsky to death at his desk in Mexico,
my classmates gasped and sat silent
beneath their hair

and I floated above your desk
and above his desk and above the war
we marched to protest, the revolution
we thought ourselves part of

in the slow cracking open of shells
in the protection of our skin
in the odd light of adolescence

Here is the room and the window and the face, Mrs. Ralph.

Nancy in the Face of Disaster

Monsoon of frogs
on a night road in California,
Sierra foothills,
where rain has spawned a downpour
or an updraft
of amphibians.

In the high beams, they hop
en masse
across the blacktop.

Nancy's at the wheel, keening
for the frogs she's flattened.
Her wails fracture into giggles
at the misery of each loud
pop beneath the tires.

She stops the car and drops
her face into her hands,
mid road in the cacophony
of hard rain and the squashing
of hoppers.

Ed, riding shotgun, says,
Go.

She sits.

Drive before
someone hits us, he says.

Nancy loves creatures
more than people.
So does Ed. Dogs, cats,
coyotes who threaten their cats.
They took their pet rat in
for brain surgery.

Six of us in the wagon,
in the steam of our breathing.
Hail shells the metal roof
and hops like frogs
across the asphalt.

This is plague number two,
says Ed, *just after blood. Number*
Five is livestock. Drive,
before cows start falling.

She moves us forward, slowly.
At each bump of a small
mass beneath the tires,
Nancy yowls
as if she can feel
the contact under her foot.

Pop.

You hit that one on purpose,
says Ed.

IV

They say he is the only owl remaining. I hear him at night
listening for the last of the mice and asking who *of no other owl.*

—"Morning on the Island," Carolyn Forché

Kayaking off Santa Cruz Island

for Wendy Van Norden

To enter the sea caves was to enter the maze of a brain, to
bob like a thought. At the lip, the swell set us down and
we stalled with our paddles, then rode the next wave in.
Sunlight cut into the multiple mouths of the cave in great
brushstrokes. Cave of a hundred blues. The swells raised our
heads toward the ceiling of rock and then dropped us. Sun
lit the porous walls into old-god faces, bearded by flickers
of foam. Gallery of echoes. Millennia of booms. Between
entrance and departure, sea voices entered the caves of our
ears and swirled in the snail of the cochlea. At this shoreline
where waves flowed through windows in rock, we rode in
and came out changed, our brains full of ocean.

Poem on a Stranger's Photo, Circa 1920

What did they know of Tillie and me
when we smiled for their photo,
the smiles they asked for,
and stretched our oars like wings?

In a rowboat tied
to the splintery dock, we giggled
side by side
like cradled babies,

both of us heart-faced and dark:
Tillie with her soft
winged hair and me with my tiny waist
cinched like a neck being choked,
my bloomers swelling
to bloat.

To the whiskey-head men
on the dock
we were nothing more
than cabbage worms,

promiscuous sisters who would
simper and rock.

What did they know of our secret
spheres and regrets?
What did they know of her blackouts
in the vineyard? Of street time that led us to the bughouse?
Of the men with horns who'd crossed us there?

The day was sweet and calm. They stumbled
above us on the dock. The pier, a hundred feet out

on its long row of posts, enclosed
the bay like their fantasy cage.

Lean together, they said.
Touch foreheads and smile,
they said, and we did, with
devilish niceness.

They thought their prized
boat another bed
to land us in.

They thought our communion was
with them
        and not with the sea
        and not with the cutting of rope
        and the cutting of chains.

When they stumbled toward shore
Tillie slipped out her boot knife,
sliced us loose,
        and we rowed—
        each on the wing of one oar,

our backs to the sea that we entered
        on adrenalin and muscle,
threading the pylons.

Their cussing came feeble.
Their stones fell short.

We rowed like angels taking their leave
of that country of drunkards
smelling of fish.

Boy in the Game House

Empty house at the top of a ladder.
Booth in the air above a diamond
of settled dust. A field at rest. No game
to announce. Give *us* this house—a girl and boy,
both eight. It's our ship, rocket, jet; becomes
our lookout, hideout, whatever we choose.

It's so long ago. Small town. We can choose
which empty spaces to enter, which ladders
to climb. In make-believe the girl becomes
a boy, grows sharp, hard as a diamond.
It's clear that all the fun stuff's just for boys,
so she cuts her hair short, plays ball in any game

that lets her in.   High up in our game
house the light planes. The boy and I choose
worlds until the world dims.   Until the ladder
creaks. Something sneaking toward our diamond
light. Long shadow at the door becomes
a man: tall body, soft face of a boy.

He won't speak to the girl: he wants the boy
to play. His zipper's down, his hand . . . *Become*
my new friend. Tell her to climb down the ladder.
She won't. He won't. It's murky. Another game
just for boys. I can't remember.   Try choosing
that she stays: the image fractures like a diamond's

faces. Turn it. Which plane of the diamond
is truth? Which imagined? I want the boy
untouched. Man backs down the ladder.
Girl protects her friend. I want to become
the one who saved him. I want out of this game
I couldn't even play in.   Why not just choose

one truth? Choose us both free. Boy becomes
the man he wants to be. Diamond empty. Game
over. Let me off the hook. Get us both down the ladder.

The Piazza

In the town square of his face,
there's a pool
where toddlers toss coins—
silver nickel, brass.

Nearly toppling from their throws,
the children rock side to side
like boats
to right themselves.

There's a gold dog with her red lady.
There are balloons, yellow and orange,
tethered to strollers
or the wrists of children.

And women on bicycles, of course,
in skirts. They honk
their rubber-ball handlebar horns.

There's a sea in his crenellated jowls.
The surf is a series of greetings
from Tunisia or Greece

or Rome with its fountains
where he stands in line—
a Jew during World War II—
to ask the pope to bless a book
for his fellow soldier.

There's a fountain in the voice
he's losing,

and a fountain in the mind that
drops to a low bubble
then blooms again, silver,
fanning out in wind.

The Screech Owl

Have you ever heard the whinny
of a screech owl,
at night, defending
its territory?
It's a triumphant sound—
little horse of the air.

January Thaw

Follow deer tracks through sodden
woods behind your house, just after ice
and the year's shortest day, and there's spring
with its alien face

like the friend who walks smiling toward you
in your dream
though you know she's dead
so the warmth between you
holds a cold spot at its center.

Your ghosts are more solid than you are.
They watch you
slip along the skin of the world
where nubs of crocus bump
toward a lie of sunlight.

Everything beneath you shifts
or snaps—
wet earth, dropped boughs, thick
history of leaves

and mud shows even deer
have slid, scrambling out of the gully
before they dug in with parallel hooves

and surged up
along the long
waves of their bodies.

Dusk slides down warm
among naked limbs. Quick
trespass of spring—

the way love is a trick of heat
that opens your clothes
and moves through you.

Death Window

In cross-country flight, I try to picture you, afraid I'm too
late—the rooms of your body closing. But when I arrive,
you've realized some kind of super life, your mind impossibly
sharp, your face stunning, your hair, against raised pillows,
roiling behind you like the Pacific Ocean, your skin the color
of honey when it congeals, a complicated golden white. You
are itched and afflicted by the tube up your nose and the tube
down your throat but you're holding court on your deathbed,
surrounded by people who adore you, which includes
everyone you've ever met, I think, except the lanky TV actor
who wheeled around to snap at you at Gelson's and looked,
you said, like a raptor. You turn your head to accommodate
each of us, remembering twenty-seven questions for twenty-
seven people who move in and out of your bedroom. The flat-
nosed Siamese curls into your ribs. "I've lost 50 pounds," you
say, "and my hearing aids won't stay in." Outside your room,
for the rest of us, there is endless food. Inside, they spoon you
a concoction from a blender then suck it out through your
nose. "What do you call this ritual," you ask the nurse, "this
dying ritual where they don't feed you?" You stare out at the
oblong pool, the rocks and palms, the patio on which coyotes
killed your beloved cat. "If I'm alive when it gets hot," you
say, "I'm going to put on my grandmother's swimsuit and get
into that pool."

Though dark had swung full down

and the low holler of stream become
just one of many voices
along with bug jabber, rustle,
and the ball-peen hammer of the woodpecker,

though the sun had plopped out of the sky
and starlings bunched on branches
against a still-gelling moon,

I stayed along wet stones,
the creek lit silver, catching tadpoles
on their squiggly route through shallow water
with the boy in baggy jeans
and a striped shirt that buttoned,

son of the man who mowed lawns at camp,
who drove a square, open, cart
and fixed toilets when mice fell into them
and drowned and clogged the pipes that ran
beneath the mess hall and bathrooms,

a sad, quiet boy; maybe he wore suspenders and maybe
brown boots he set on rocks with dark socks
stuffed in them. He had a pail, I'm sure of that,

and with our pants rolled up we stepped
barefoot through the creek on slippery rocks,
snagging tadpoles in their orbit, not for any torture
some other boy might have
dreamed up, but just to cup the squirmy,
snot-body things in our hands
and let them swirl in our bucket, dark mass in moonlight,

before we slid them back into the eddies
of the moving creek.

I forgot where I was supposed to be—
the cramped cabin with the girls
in short sets who could keep their shoes
clean and never lose things—

I forgot the blocks of time that corralled us,
and the riding of bored horses in a line
who stopped and started as a line,
one horse's nose against the next one's butt,
who had no use for my perfect neck reining.

At the creek with the boy who
sometimes rode in the cart with his father,
I waded among quivering
tadpoles and felt the stream ripple
between my toes

until counselors formed a band and carried
flashlights and called and called for us
across the darkened woods.

West Virginia

in memory of Chuck Kinder

Because the day is warm
and sweet with breeze,
and because I won't be driving anywhere
any time soon,

I think of you and how I'd think of you
when I drove south

because you asked me once,
did I notice how the air turned
just a little sweeter
when I crossed the border
into West Virginia?

And did I roll down my windows,
breathe it in
crank up some Lucinda
and floor the pedal?

And just like that I became
the outlaw you'd invented.
No longer the reliable, uncoddled
daughter of the humid
heart of the country.

No. I was a lipstick-faced adventurer,
my past a little bluer
a little redder
than most would guess,

a knife stashed in my boot,
chased by demons of intriguing origin,
barreling across the state line.

Little House of Steel

There's a roasting pot
in the shape of a house
heavy and silver
a roof built for snow
with weathervane handle

pot of an old-world kitchen
kitchen of candles and glass
kitchen of lemon
of linen
of light through an open window

kitchen of linger
of lime, of a long line
of broad-shouldered women
young broads in the rupture of nations
the deportations

split the towns
split the houses
split the women

Cross the ocean
Slap the cards on the table
and puff your Pall Malls
filter less
Nisht geferlech
Gott im Himmel
Nu? You should live so long

So long, Aunt Rose of the spicy mouth,
Aunt Anna, Aunt May

Aunt Bell of the two-toned hair
bell of the family
of the husbands one, two, three

So long, so long

And yet
the oddness of the house pot
its cool-hammered heft

too pretty for peas
too heavy for lifting

toward the finely set table
of smuggled crystal

table of lace, of glass
table of borrowed children

Little house of silver
too small to protect you.

L'Autoroute

If I run out of options,
I'll go back to the highway
between Paris and Calais

where a caravan of small trucks
hauling radishes and cabbage
in latticed wood crates

stopped at midnight to pick up
the French boy and me. We slept
like two cucumbers beside the crated

vegetables, against the wood-slat
walls of truck bed. At each stop we woke
to unload produce in the dark

handed off to men in suspenders
with rolled-up sleeves
and cigarettes stuck to their lips,

to be stacked in garages and sheds
in small towns. This work
earned us passage to the hovercraft.

And on the dark road behind us,
a world spooled out, forever perishing.
What the truckers said to us was

Stay. Live here with us.
We offer you vegetables.
We offer you this life.

And if someone had put a key
in my hand, I would have
carried it past middle age

as it seems I have, as it seems I've gone
back to that night when I need it.